WIZARD

OF

WOMAN

Extracts From Journals Collated Since 1977

Bruce Charles Kirrage

PITTSBURGH, PENNSYLVANIA 15238

The contents of this work including, but not limited to, the accuracy of events, people, and places depicted; opinions expressed; permission to use previously published materials included; and any advice given or actions advocated are solely the responsibility of the author, who assumes all liability for said work and indemnifies the publisher against any claims stemming from publication of the work.

This is a work of fiction. It does not represent any person, place, or event, past, present or future.

RoseDog Books
585 Alpha Drive
Suite 103
Pittsburgh, PA 15238
Visit our website at www.rosedogbookstore.com

ISBN: 978-1-4809-6424-2
eISBN: 978-1-4809-6447-1

Contents

▲▼▲

▲▼▲

▲▼▲

24
(Hoops and Shovels)

Twenty-four roses for twenty-four hours a day
Thats the one and only way
Two me higher than the sun
You mine hey hey hey

Twenty-four roses for twenty-four hours I say
You are the one and only OK
To take through slime and mud
You here stay stay stay

Twenty-four roses for twenty-four hours in clay
Thats for you one I day every way
Two a way and then done
You be here away they they

Alpha 1

Up and down again
Beset by a beta creature
Defying confusion
This illusion
Why does an alpha rhythm
Paradoxically traverse a mountain terrain
Odds of hundred to one
By those with statistical leaning
Doubtless to know feel and see
Compressing juggling
With word and sign
Number and meaning
Thirty per cent chance
Or more to expect
Ten per cent
With the greatest respect
Lean to erect

Alpha 2

Why does an Alpha man's rhythm
Paradoxically traverse a mountain
Up and then down again
Beset a Beta creature
Defying confusion
Defying illusion
Odds of hundred to one
By those with a statistical leaning
Doubtless to know how to feel and see
A comprehensive juggling
With word sign and number
Thirty per cent chance or more can expect
Ten per cent chance or more
With the greatest of respect
Ten per cent chance
To stand among the best erect

Alzheimers

Why so slow
This memory lag
Why the brain
Like some old hag

An Angelic Eagle at Summer

Meadow lie unfallow
Winter bunting crow carrow
Come eglect not regret
For want and get
Fallow the farrow
Further intoward narrow

B

XXXX me B
XXXX me with your ash-blond silver hair
XXXX me right there
XXXX me B
XXXX me like an angel
XXXX me from above
XXXX me B
XXXX me with your love
XXXX me B
XXXX me anyway
XXXX me do not stop
XXXX me till I drop
XXXX me B
XXXX me everywhere
XXXX me B
XXXX me the young widow you are
XXXX me to death

Bells Below

Man-made day
Delivered report
Query words with which to say
All on your marks
Sympathy No-No-No
And a working-class brother elsewhere Ho-Ho-Ho
Cunningly contrive of a plan to dissociate
An older long lost man
To ruminate
Who would dance to their tune
Can-can itching about
Passing criticism
Two-tongued man
Why so slow this memory lag
Why the brain
Like some old hag
Like some old hag
Doubt that
Dirty sole
Dirty rat
Enquire within
The cause of my infernal sin
In my minds word
Get out of pain
Down from some sodden cloud
As stupid fool

Think
Better now
Sound hear
Actor yet seer

Between Us and Them

A patient
Stood in front
Who was arguing
Angrily arguing his want
Consultant in double trouble
No one nearby at all
What could he say
Who could he call
Look flashed across his face
Fear once started difficult to erase
Before very long had quickly grown
Fear like that I too had known
What to do moved then
Stand between patient and doctor
Between us and them
With a door nearby
Opened wide
The doctor slid through
Safety guaranteed
Now inside

Birds and Bees

The birds and bees are around
The bees fly just above the ground
Let it be
To you and to me

How do I recover
How do I juxtapose
From what I suppose

How can I escape
Yet remain within the fold
What is my nature
Why believe what I am told

You are a reflection of my soul
I calmly said
Her eyes swivelled left and right
To what dim-distant thought
I know not yet

Despite the angle of her limbs by day
What time-honoured machine
At night was at play

The two betwixt one and one more yet
The riddle before me

Let it be
To you and to me

Even the little beetle at rest on my knee
I knocked kindly off
To play in the grass
For another day
As happy as a child
With a new won Wii

Black Singing

Hark sweet words of youth
From yonder fair to dark
Wander not as a cloud
Is a tiny noise loud

Blank Verse

Blank verse should be
Sane without riling
Bit by bit without tat
Free as a bird
Earned and studied and as
New as a good plate of food

Celebration Generation

This is a song
And goes like this
Have you got the gist

A song of celebration
For the younger generation
Burp Hip and Twist

Now this little song
For you we call along
For you we sing

Four verses of song
To you we belong
To do our thing

Chip

There was a chip
Went to market
Not too bright
Returned months later
Saying I am the light
To lighten the darkness
Speak to the tiny machine
It clothes you and me
Tells the answer
To two plus three
Never mind your mistake
The problem
It will correct 'em

Confidence

Let me try and gain a little confidence
Said the ant to the elephant
If I crawl under your big foot
Will you tread on me

Contentment

To be alone
Yet not feel lonely
And being lonely
Yet not feel alone

Daughter of Angie and Den

Comprehensive understanding of women and men
Do to think
Have instead a little drink
Say you suffer who what when

Day and Night

In the cold light of day
A poem seems far away
But in the dead of night
Imagination takes flight

Dog-leg Runner

Tyres squeeling
Hands hold tight
On steering wheeling right

Round corner
Up straight
Cannot wait

Now see glaring back at me
As some bear
Woken from lair

Drifting

Drifting as a piece of wood
With a heart on fire
Tripped up by an unseen wire
Now drowning in the flame
With feelings of shame

Education

It may be said
I should have read
Books by Marx Engels or Frew-ed
This odd thought
Adds little comfort
To my mind
To overcome the confusion I find
However any rhyme
Like time
May help rediscover
Real love of her

EHA

An EHA was on its way
I awoke startled
In disarray
Excruciating pain within my chest
Struggled downstair
Slumped in a chair
Text her then and there
Drink coffee
Walk around
Her only reply
I'll try I'll try

Elizabeth the Second (W)

I grind with my mind
The thought that does bind
Try as I might
You are right
With or without you
I still the fight
About the one in the seat
Again to you I repeat
Your walk as you leave
Left me in little doubt discover
You love someone or other

Engine
(Suck and Blow)

This gotta be good boys
You should have seen it suck
Moved and blew
A Chu-Chu

Steam coming from its ears
As it worked its way along the track
That rippling flesh and steel-capped engine
Front to back

Let's hit the sack boys la...la...la
Let's ease the pain boys la...la...la
Let's go insane boys la...la...la

Euphemism

A spade is a spade
Or is it not
Why all the innocent chatter
What is the real difference
Whether murdered by lead
Or chemical matter

Or do I miss the point of all war
Or have I forgot
To take out an enemy position
Surely means
Kill the lot

The point of euphemism must be
To sanitise unclean thought
Replace with another
More palatable to you and me

Expected

Life's so short
Why not slow it down a bit
And we will savour things done and felt
Remember places and people
Who accept reject nectered

Saying what people will believe
I am the light
To lighten the darkness
Please speak to this machine
Clothe you and me
It will tell you the answer to two plus three
Never mind your mistake
It will correct yee

Face Your Fear

Dry your tear
Remember remember remember
Two thousand and eight October November and December
Are we just players on this planet
Eating life as a gannet
With bottle cheese and whine
Help me through this anguished time
It's life sting at me
So much worse than a bee
What is going on inside my head
Am I alive or am I dead
If I ignore the while
What then - how to beguile
What is this adult world
A man without his girl
The expression the mother
What is this or love of her
How do I discover love
From way way way above
If it's madness out of sight
Pedro Calderon De La Barca is right
What if Pedro is wrong
Logic reason defy this song
How do I again bang my gong
Be someone somewhere all along
Start once more to relive
For in every word I do give

Finite My Night Kite

Down doing night
Inside sight
Finite my Night Kite
Wherewithal to say
Multicoloured way

Down is ride
Inside hide
Finite my Night Kite
Go to where day by day
Our simple way

Between side to side
Inside died
Finite my Night Kite
Straight to over and again
Whereto by brain

Chorus~
Mix it betwixt our clan
Say to me
This is nit
Mount Tho View
Man be

Forty-Five Years

A mad barking as a dog world
Pillful Dutiful Pityful
Then as if by magic - me
Split from stem to stern
No longer a minion
But a man able to earn

Something had happened
It blew my mind
Then was it magic - you
Incomprehensible tough - as hard as nails
Left the scene
While I was off the rails

Doubtless all three have loved others
I am sure it is true
Through and through

Getting at the Truth

A politician reading out his speech
To an audience he wants to reach
A soldier his only right
The ability to stay the fight
A doctor trying to listen
To a patients' words
Ramblings and driven
A young man
He cannot hear
Truth from afar
And truth from near

Getting Better

How why who what and when
Oh as a baby now and then
You have my sum of all parts within my pen
If nothing is all else a monkeyed zoo
Why you top to toe do
If love is only divine
Pray shackle my self to the moneyed isle
If everything is and yet what for
How am I to love you
I implore yet more
As images sounds visions appear
Its you I cry here

Grand Old Munster Muncher

The Grand Old Munster Muncher of Wunster
Beckoned three maids while confirming them
As they knelt seeking God
He excited his rod
And pumped his seminal dream in them

Half-Cut-N-Half-Cussed

Half-cut-n-half-cussed by some medicine man
I do what I can
I am as I sit
I write about it

Paying only half attention
Glance up in front of me
Subtitles from a TV

No one knows grammar
Or how to spell
I live alone in half home
Half hell

My other half long-gone
Outshone by some new crazy half-light
That too has dimmed
Taken flight

Why pay heed to an In-law-brother
Why persuade almost every other

Why was I not right
What should I believe
Was there a vested interest
With an axe to grind

▲▽▲

Only half-cut
Only half-blind
I will likely know only the half of it
I only lost half my mind

Now arguably half the man I was
In some physical pain
No one will completely understand
How fate played its hand
How it shaped half my life
Ripped away loyalty
Fane trust and a wife

What is our destiny
What can we perceive
An extension of our own reality
All we can do for posterity
Is a concept to conceive

Compassion Courage Understanding
Truth Interpretation
Humour too
Is it this that binds us all together
Or should we just talk
Contemplate the weather

How do I unlock the banana of life
Look with awe to the past
While I can
As I am
Half-monkey
Half-man

How do I gain
How to fight the need
Power lust money and greed

Have I already completed evolution's task
Have I done everything I was asked
What next now
Who
When
Where
Why and
How

In melancholy mood I contemplate
How long before I begin to pass
Half-way through that gate
Expect on my tombstone writ
Was that really it

Hardwick

A man called Hardwick
Who by a cricket ball was struck
Inscribed on his tombstone
Were three words
Hardwick hard-boiled hard-luck

Horse Flies

Horse Flies Aurora - No Horse Flies.
Be Pegasus (Per Gases).
Horse Flies Be Pegasus (Per Gaseous)
No Flies On This Horse Lasts

Therein speaker
Sometime courage poorer richer
Sometime aurora light
Number even letter fourer

Under hour roofs catch
Need two nest lie most
Apres petit mort
Amore hatch lay toast

Heart ash hair
Black dressed back
Give luck unexcusable
Within laugh's sack

Delight moreover
Plover lids front rim
Stroke kindly caressing
Within beyond swim

▲▽▲

Both yet somehow desist
Till inner rimmed does yell
Knot entwined lustful
Kelly's gell

Hear move soothe
Liken well litttle thirst
Come listen music
Swelling curse emptying burst

Shut upon
Hit me there slam
Grow grow grow
Tightly hold inner clam

Faster two as art
Use as fulsome riding
Ongoing logging into gear
Slipping piece sliding

Then show
Till no pill box made wise
Noisily riding cantering galloping
Horse flies

Make again blather
Thither that
Cup for later
Stood two sat

Fane strength ride
Make me wend bit
Hurt pain riddle
And ever yet end fit

Ne'er forget yet forever
Do again main
Stoney hell unwin
Allow life wax wain

Let's view lark
Dribble around bell
Play rest play
Herein all well

Only itself free last
Drive wedge Trigger life mile
Living happening loving
Perchance long while

How to Love

Love not only with the eyes
But with work and grind
Of hand body mind

It's Me Funkey

Drives a wedge through to the dock of a horses ....
..... Arise
Breathe sharply act wise
Horses are black or somewhere in between
God help you before ice-cream
Beget me nine fifteen
Once forgotten always seen
Done dusted cream dream
For dyke
Go for hike
Bike

King of the Road

Know cards
Know booze
Know pets
Ain't got no flannelettes
Ah but two hours of pushing broom
Buys an eight by four
Three bedroom

Know What is the Matter

What are we
Stardust
Compared to vast space
An insignificant dot no matter a human race

Where are we going
Nowhere
Just around and around
Within a huge vacuum silently no sound

How long will we last
Forever
If we believe
Science tells us not we are born die and grieve

Why do we think
Searching for universal truths
Beyond our sky
That is why

Why do we suffer
Born and die so alone
Within our own pain
Yet lonely not it is our gain

▲▽▲

The answer is between our deepest depths
Betwixt our matter
Amid somewhere way way way above
To music and to love

Ladder

Across and up the synapse
We are diverse
We are the messengers
Of hope with verse

As seeing mother earth
Since from before our birth
Seeing our mother - streuth
Beauty a complexity and a truth

And you my baby plover
Bestest lover
Discover truth - my lonely
Absent one and only

Letting You Into My Heart

Through your eyes accustom to see
Thereby judge a betterment in me
A chance fane happiness
Understanding wealth
Yet above all else
Good health

With a jug jug jugglin'
Cuddlin'
Feeling touching wooing
Cooing
A changeling yet from ruin

Life Living

Tenuous health
Tenuous peace of mind

Dim memory.... ability....question
Answer.... doubt....passion

For out to sea
A notion

Yet the island of certainty
Can we find

Love and the riddle unwind
Like an old clock

Time slow down
Today has its own history

Tomorrow its own reflection
Then some peace

For the essence of gratification
Decision can be hard

Either yes or no
To an outright action

▲▼▲

Change the future
And change reaction

With a pill or drug
To mend a broken heart

With a Chekhov spirit
And yet not too unkind

That is all we have
It seems

And need to live life
With love not bought

With labour and strife
With much thought

You turn around
And Life done

Life's Short

I hear you say
Tomorrow is just another day
But then today
For its own
History
Tomorrow a recollection
Foray Peace Hope
Dare Gratification

Love of the First God

There was a man from Mars
Whose pen shaped like a vase
So he dipped it in
Till was inked well within
Now instead of hating
There are flowers

Lovers Delight

To lie out in the heather
On a moonlit night
The taste of coffee
In the morning light

Baby rings on fingers
And much more
Add to my only lover's delight

Loves Song

What's in a song
What's in a poem
The rhythms of life
For all to know 'em

Madness

Get Schizophrenia
You'll never be alone
Get bipolar
Opposites incontrovertibly
Get Mr & Mrs Average
Get the great unwashed
Get dementia
Forget everything

Mars Two

There once woman from Mars
Whose planet shaped like jars
So dipped in
Till inked well within
Instead of hating
There flowers

Math Sum - Question Why
(Over the Event Horizon)

Why does a math sum seem to be firstly
Incomprehensible - a curse and worsely
Not to rhyme
Or have the right aversely

Money

Turn evil around
What have we got
Live of course have we not
Therein is found the hidden agenda
Money what

So I heard with dismay
Bribes had been taken
By the noblest profession
Had stooped so low
From their confession

To gain advantage
Over his peers
Everyman has his price
Or so it appears
And places his greedy heart
On the altar of vice

Mood

Of mood here I brood
My heads a quake
I need a golden hand-shake
Once or twice
Between the vice
Of spirit
And water
A do-do
Oughta
Cha-Cha
Blow me down with a feather
I can if you can
Said the Toucan

Morning in Winter in England

Sleep until dawn
Then suddenly awake
Jump out of bed
Soak my head

Yet I begin to shake
With such gloom
From cold and fear
So little cheer

I soon walk on solemnly
Now and then
Cast my eye
Above to the cold grey sky

However slowly with some satisfaction
Realise that
Life is not too bad
Now somewhat better even glad

Mum

Mum was her name
And so she was and always is
An actress by choice
And will always be
A Mum above all else
A real Mum to me

She did say
To me one day
What shall we do
Turn you upside down
You can be a broom
(To the edge of doom)

Narcissus

A picture by Van Gogh
A portrait of self-love
A mixed up vanity
And final loss of sanity

No Borders Crossed

This is what it seemed
This is what I know
This is what I had gleaned

A young female walks across
To innocently sit on my knee
She is gently ushered away
Away from me

Too much familiar tone
With firm yet polite rebuff
Is clinically stopped in its track
That is quite enough

Good heavens
Never to be allowed or to look back
It is well documented and well known
Or led quickly to the sack

Having been some say
It is very obvious to me
That the only place to be
Is somewhere in the middle do you see

Number Seven

An unusual old man - number seven
Asked can a fellow go to heaven
Pass go
Smile a while
Bless yo'

Opposite

You cannot have heaven
Without knowing hell

You cannot know illness
Without first being well

You cannot know goodness
Without first being bad

You cannot be wise
Unless first a fool
Sit in a corner
Dunce on a stool

These opposites of life
May simply be
Life's rich pagentry
Incontrovertibly

Pain

I think therefore I am
I am therefore I exist
I exist therefore I live
I live therefore I do
I do therefore write

I rummage around in my black-bag head
Finding more words to what I have said
Its stranger pain
Leader
Ignorant of stain
Now it can hurt so much
Medicine is no crutch

Passion

It's easy to make the facts fit the description
Of Bipolar addiction
The truth and
The schizoid crazy passion of youth

Peace of Mind

Some harmony
Music
Chance to relax
Chance to unwind
Gain a little
Peace of mind

Peace
(written to and for the Yazidi)

Wholly grumble on the floor
Who can watch over yore
What likens thus and thee
Wherefore wherever whenever
Plastered goosed lambed
Forever better be

Perfection

Bless you since heaven time
Has shown it was not best to be alone
A partner suited to my mind

Solitarily, pleased kind thing
Who may always see
A betterment to the world in me
And slightly by my own humble side
Fane happiness, splendour, wealth and pride

Pill

Still here now
Controlled by the pill
Helped
Within our lost will

Poor cow
You and I
In a world of the pill
Sunshine in the sky

God up above
Not anymore
People now love
Are you sure

Politic of Stigma

What can be done
What can be said
While the politics of stigma
Run through the head

Who has most to lose
Who has most to gain
While the politics of stigma
Cause so much pain

A name rhymes with pine and sine
A February day in the year
While the politics of stigma
Are hidden right here

What does Pine to Sine mean
What did it convey
While the politics of stigma
Cause confusion disarray

Why does this happen
Why do I not understand
While the politics of stigma
Grow secretly underhand

▲▼▲

Why not want to know
Why do lovers never want to sense
While the politics of stigma
Condemn hope o'er experience

Why therein melancholy
Like a lonely friend found
While the politics of stigma
Rage above and underground

Power Lust Money Greed

Have I already completed evolution task
Have I done everything I was asked
What next now
Who
When
Where
Why and
How

In melancholy mood I contemplate
How long before I begin to pass
Half-way through that gate
Expect on my tombstone writ
Was that really it
Half-wit

Power of Poetry

Why is a poem so powerful
With its inner sound
Belongs to its beat
With the rhythm too
Can hammer out a message
For me and you

Writers forced to say something important
Now in tune
Turned condensed by the discipline
Rambling thought
From their heart and head
Into something what ought

Prayer

Even temperament
And our will cease
With all our strength of purpose
We only lease

Body and mind
In youth
Is able to write a lot about sex
A self-charged asset it directs

There is no sequel to its equal
............Love
If there is I'll grab its horns
And not let go e'en till day dawns

Prisoner in My Own Hind

What likens thus and thee
Bar none
Then happiness grasped
Plastered goosed lambed
Snatched away
Broken in mind
Body
Forever better be
(spirit desolate)
Crying and totally alone
Black nothingness
Complacency peace mental/physical illness
Shootings of zebras
Wholly grimble
On the floor
Who can watch o'er yore
Five term nor

Psycho-Chems

A chemical castration
Desire undone the solution
Drug distribution
Normality aim and conclusion

The patient gives a hefty kick
With this supposed death-defying trick
No drink about
Senses routed out

Personality hidden
Watched and forbidden
Money - no it's not his needing
Just weeding

Begins to speak needs
Do more deeds
Slowly at first
Develops a hunger - a thirst

Right the wrong
Discovers what was there all along
Music, love and even he
Can start to bang his wi

Quetiapine
(Tablet contradiction)

It's no sin
Take the damn thing
It's not cruel
To be so over-ruled

Am I well
Or am I ill
Don't know
Take the Quetiapine pill

Want to watch TV
Sit around all day
Take Quetiapine
There's no better way

Am I too fat
And not thin
Don't matter
Take your Quetiapine

Need a loving woman
Feeling lonely or mad
Take the rubbish
You've just been had

▲▼▲

Think you're clever
Or feeling down
Take Quetiapine
Half-blind in love clown

Could go on and on
While remember Valentine
As writing this song
While taking Quetiapine

Inner Self:

Quote

`Louder than a thought
yet lower than a voice'
That's what she is....

Quote
(for America)

Is like the stars that arc across the night sky
Incence us so we regroup

Quote

Love And Madness

'When love is not madness
It is not lov'
Attributed to
Pedro Calderon De La Barca

Quote

Morning of an After-life

'What we perceive is an extension of our own reality.
What we do take our own courage, compassion,
understanding, and truth of interpretation'

Reflection
(On Peaceful Humours)

Reflect on love
Fed-up or profound
Disturbed or unwound
Comerbound

With dove a carrier
Across a space of infinite thought
Yet can be ought
Sought

Seeing a vision of hope
Alternate with nothing
How frothing
Good evening

Renting in Poverty (1980's)

Am I sane or maybe not
Nothing on but what I got

Four candles burning
And Calor gas flame
One shirt drying
With M & S name

Am cold to the bone
Too full to complain
Living here
To prove I'm still sane

Sitting here
I've been too doped to do much
'Cept stay here
No Lord Such

Electric and water are off
Landlord don't care
Landline don't work
Thinks I'm nuts should be back there

Me....I'm felt like death walking
His wife's the same
Somebody please just wave

Are so urbane

Prove I'm still needed
Yet no fuss no bother
Fed up as I am
Crikey anyone seen mother

Rook

(Space Flight to Mars)

Our space as to
Alight a chemical feather
No air
No disgrace
Darker energy
Matter or race
Whither that energy
Right place

Respect and reflect
Arise, cough or choke not
A lost shoe and lace
As mirror to your soul
Your eyes a blank stare
Your whole
Your grace

Rooms or Space
(Incarceration)

53 up a tree

54 bang the door

Female side open wide

Everything that opens and closes

38 get it straight

Simply put

Well then

Just wait

Till sparrows minus one

I do I am done

A Zorastrian

Rugby
(Public Schooling)

Broken nose

Knock out

From head to toes

Few days unconscious in bed

He'll be OK

So they said

Much got wrong

Life trouble

Reflective song

Schizomers (Brain Thinking) Money

Ask quietly
All I get is what I thought
Why rye lie
Sport thought tort taught

Is this the way
Integrity unknown
Money clone
Repeat known

Secret

Is there a part of me
That I should hide
One of selfishness and pride

Is there a part of me
That I should not speak
One of boorishness
That goes over the peak

Is there a part of me
That I cannot ignore
The present and future
And all that has gone before

If all these parts were out of sight
Would it could it make it right

Sixty-one

Drugged yet sober
Out in the cold
Sixty-one years old

Somewhat mad bad and sad
Out in the cold
Sixty-one years old

No more consider young
Out in the cold
Sixty-one years old

Solitude beckons friendless
Out in the cold
Sixty-one years old

Ex-wife sons far away
Out in the cold
Sixty-one years old

Where is my home
Out in the cold
Sixty-one years old

Snakes and Ladders

An enigma from Mars
Nothing there nil without repeachement
Contemplated flowers in a vase
Should work construe paths
Up and onward to each pole

And within reflection
Left to be alone that sole
Do as would be oughta
Swirling around by water
Without all around arias

Make complex and fully whole
Looking towards and after
Should help as a starter
Made helpful and artier

Eat meat vegetable make heartier
Will go further and lead three
Onward for no less as Vee
Happier and with laughter

Song to Hozier

Birds above
Flowers below
Sing to me
No Song of Solomon
Just me
You and I
Have been as high
As kite
And low
As low can be
Zee and I
Come no high
Lower and
Lower
Down down
Middle around
Till quiet
Little sound

Speech

If thought
Ought
Then surely
Utter
Matter

Stubbornness

It started soon after your mother conceived
Oh really I replied relieved
You have an unrepentant stomach tract
Is that a fact
I guessed it was a pill or two
Made me do the things I do

Syria Et Al

Of Syria those same
Where there flee
Birth death and maim
Trouble struggle
One end should never be
Death dust amid dirty rubble

Terrorism
(More Will Rise Up and Defeat You)

If you only know terrorism
How will you win
With what schism

Use peace as your lance
Make your fortune and luck owed to
Coincidence and chance

A coincidence to redeem
A chance to heal
A wisdom without the scream

War let it fail
Peace is easier
Then let it prevail

Instead fill that state
With the joy that you are
Without the rage and the hate

Let me be the fool
And gaze in wonder
Now at you so cool

Theology
(An Anthology)

It's not just we climbing
Mountains to stars
Or as single pebbles on beach
But from child's first cry
Trying trying trying to reach
To air above
Amid depths despair
Find peace hope love

Unconditional Lover
(Jesus Christ)

I grind with my mind
With thought that does bind

Try as I may or with might
Your are right

With or without you
I fight too

About the one in seat
I repeat

Leave little doubtless discovery
With thee lovery

Universal Serendipity and Truth

Again resposibility
Awareness of history
Good intention
With compassion
Amount of gain
Given sane
Truth
Until death
Streuth
Happiness justice benevolence
Careful handling
Zesting understanding
Sense and recompense

Wedding
(1988)

In sunny St. Lucia
A day long ago
On a beach drenched by sea and sand
In a little gazebo

It was November `88
Really beautiful no less
You looked really great
In your inexpensive white Richards dress

You caressed by a moonlit night
Carried you along that beach
You are now so far away
Now out of reach

What Comes...

What come from the pen of The Specialist Hat
Comes to me now
This and that

What comes to the pen of The Specialist Mind
Drugged & confined
Comes to me now
Hearty and kind

What comes to the pen of The Specialist Other
Is no bother
Rather and over
Said more more
Said the claw
Of the Devils Hand
A sing-a-long band
Aforementioned and over our land
Send the mad mind
Repeated as yet
Before I see
The very deed
This Fortuitous seed

You Were

Was thirty-eight
Had to wait
Could not up sticks
Could not play those tricks
Desisted
Your computer to fix
Looking fine
Red wine
Was naughty
Gone to heaven
Number seven
Turned loose
Silly as a goose
Always so much…
Bees in a hive

Young Man for Stamboul

A worried young man from Stamboul
Discovered a red spot on his tool
Said the Doctor a cynic
Get out of my clinic
Wipe off the lipstick
You fool

Zestful Life Living

Crow
Hoe
Z

Zestfulness

Why its best

Little confidence gets bigger
Carries on and on
Somewhat like reproduction

Little confidence
Can pick you up again
Like yo-yo
Always bouncing back
Now you have the knack

Little confidence
Can instil peace of mind
Harmony of music
Chance to relax
And unwind

Lightning Source UK Ltd.
Milton Keynes UK
UKHW020802030522
402417UK00009B/505